# SESAME STREET

## WELCOMING WORDS

# WELCOME TO SPANISH
## with SESAME STREET

## J. P. PRESS

Lerner Publications ◆ Minneapolis

**Dear Parents and Educators,**

From its very beginning, *Sesame Street* has promoted mutual respect and cultural understanding by featuring a cast of diverse and lovable characters. *Welcome to Spanish* introduces children to the wonderful, wide world we live in. In this book *Sesame Street* friends present handy and fun vocabulary in a language kids may not know. These words can help young readers welcome new friends. Have fun as you explore!

Sincerely,

The Editors at Sesame Workshop

# Table of Contents

## WELCOME! 4

Count It! 28

**Rosita's Favorite Words** 30

**Further Information** 31

# WELCOME!

¡Bienvenido!
(Say BYEN-veh-
NEE-doh)

## How to Speak Spanish

Practice speaking Spanish! Each word is broken up into sounds called syllables. Do you see the syllable in CAPITAL LETTERS? That's the sound you emphasize the most!

Hello.
**Hola.**
OH-la

**This is Abelardo.
He lives in Mexico.**

# What is your name?
## ¿Cómo te llamas?
KOH-moh teh YAH-mahs


# My name is . . .
## Me llamo . . .
meh YAH-moh . . .

Me llamo
Abby.

# friendship
## amistad
ah-mees-tahd

# Will you be my friend?
## ¿Quieres ser mi amigo?
KYEHR-ays sehr
mee ah-MEE-goh

You're my best friend!

¡Eres mi mejor amigo!

# Meet my family!

## ¡Conoce a mi familia!

koh-NOH-say ah mee
fah-MEE-lee-ah

**dad**
**papá**
pah-PAH

**mom**
**mamá**
mah-MAH

**brother**
**hermano**
**ehr-MAH-noh**

**sister**
**hermana**
**ehr-MAH-nah**

**grandma**
**abuela**
**ah-BWAY-lah**

**grandpa**
**abuelo**
**ah-BWAY-loh**

**Thank you.**
**Gracias.**
GRAH-see-ahs

**You are welcome.**
**De nada.**
deh NAH-dah

12

**Please.**
**Por favor.**
pore fah-VORE

**I'm sorry.**
**Lo siento.**
loh see-EHN-toh

breakfast
**desayuno**
des-ah-YOO-noh

lunch
**almuerzo**
ahl-MWEHR-soh

snack
**refrigerio**
reh-free-HEH-ree-oh

dinner
**cena**
SEH-nah

# I'm thirsty.
**Tengo sed.**
TEHN-goh SED

# I'm hungry.
**Tengo hambre.**
TEHN-goh HAHM-bray

**Cookie Monster hungry.**

**Cookie Monster tiene hambre.**

How are you?
¿Cómo estás?
KOH-moh ehs-TAHS

I'm fine, thank you.
Estoy bien, gracias.
ehs-TOY BYEHN GRAH-see-ahs

I like you.
**Me agradas.**
meh ah-GRAH-dahs

Elmo loves you.
**Elmo te quiere.**

ELMO

**happy**
contento
cohn-TEN-toh

**grumpy**
**malhumorado**
**mal-oo-more-ADOH**

**proud**
**orgulloso**
or-goo-YOH-soh

**excited**
**emocionado**
eh-moh-see-oh-NAH-doh

**dog**
**perro**
PEH-roh

**animals**
**animales**
ah-nee-MAHL-ehs

**fish**
**pez**
PESS

**bird**
**pájaro**
PAH-ha-roh

**cat**
**gato**
GAH-toh

I like animals.

Me gustan los animales.

# colors
## colores
coh-LOH-rehs

**My favorite color is . . .**
**Mi color favorito es . . .**
mee cohl-OR
fah-vore-EE-toh
ess . . .

red
**rojo**
ROH-ho

orange
**naranja**
nah-RAHN-hah

yellow
**amarillo**
ah-mah-REE-yoh

green
**verde**
VEHR-deh

blue
**azul**
ah-ZOOL

purple
**púrpura**
POOR-poo-rah

Let's play!
¡Juguemos!
hoo-GAY-mohs

toys
juguetes
hoo-GEH-tehs

What do you like to do?
¿Qué te gusta hacer?
kay teh GOO-stah
ah-SEHR

We love to learn.
Nos encanta
aprender.

Goodbye.
**Adiós.**
ah-DEEOS

See you soon!
**¡Hasta pronto!**
AH-stah PROHN-toh

# Count It!

**1** one
**uno**
OO-noh

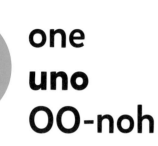

**2** two
**dos**
DOHS

**3** three
**tres**
TREHS

**4** four **cuatro** KWAH-tro

**5** five **cinco** SEEN-koh

**6** six **seis** SAYSS

**7** seven **siete** see-EH-teh

**8** eight **ocho** OH-cho

**9** nine **nueve** noo-EH-veh

**10** ten **diez** dee-ESS

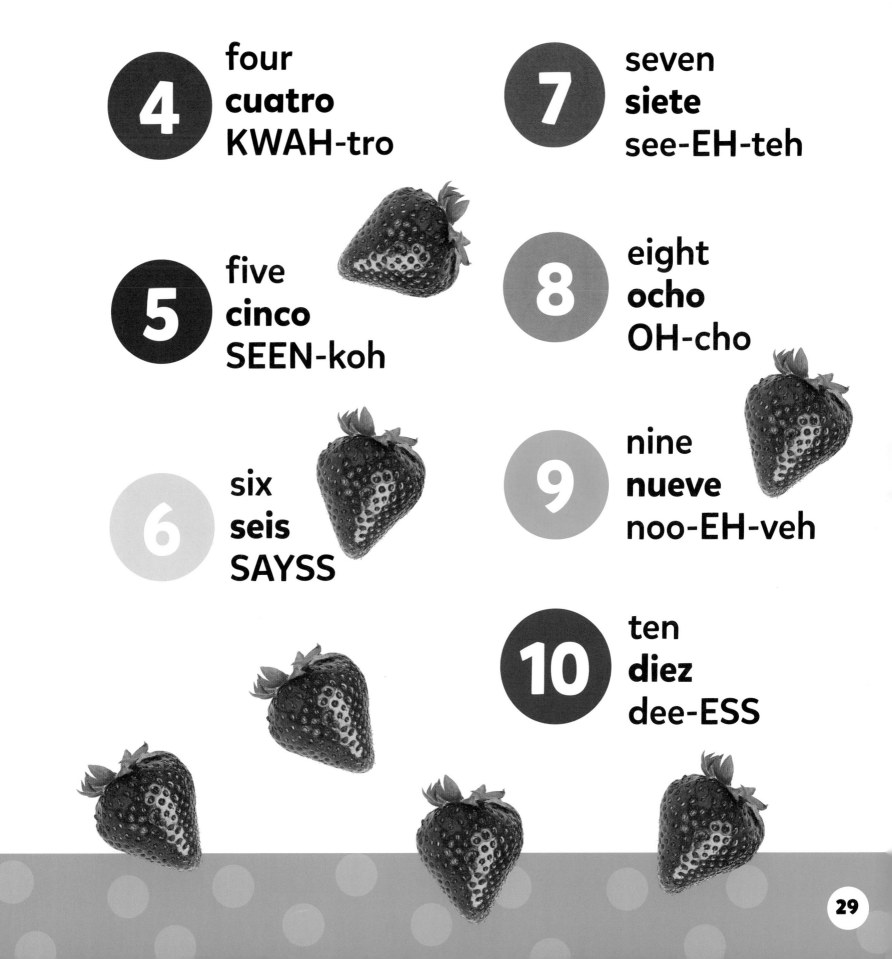

# Rosita's Favorite Words

I love music!
¡Me encanta
la música!

singing
**cantar**
cahn-TAHR

**guitar**
**guitarra**
ghee-TAH-rah

# Further Information

Atlantic, Leonard. *¡A hacer deportes! / We Play Sports!* New York: Gareth Stevens, 2018.

Graubart, Norman D. *Mi perro / My Dog*. New York: PowerKids, 2014.

Hutchins, J. *Spanish First Words=Primera Palabras en Español*. New York: Scholastic, 2013.

Online Free Spanish: A Fun Way to Learn Spanish
https://onlinefreespanish.com/

PBS Kids: Oh Noah!
http://pbskids.org/noah/index.html

Sesame Street
http://www.sesamestreet.org

Lerner Publications Company
An imprint of Lerner Publishing Group, Inc.
241 First Avenue North
Minneapolis, MN 55401 USA

For reading levels and more information, look up this title at
www.lernerbooks.com.

Main body text set in Mikado.
Typeface provided by HVD.

Additional image credits: ESB Professional/Shutterstock.com, p. 20 (dog);
clarst5/Shutterstock.com, p. 20 (bird); Eric Isselee/Shutterstock.com, p. 20 (cat);
Gunnar Pippel/Shutterstock.com, p. 20 (fish); Super Prin/Shutterstock.com, p. 23
(butterfly).

**Library of Congress Cataloging-in-Publication Data**

Names: Press, J. P., 1993– author. | Children's Television Workshop, contributor.
Title: Welcome to Spanish with Sesame Street / J. P. Press.
Other titles: Sesame Street (Television program)
Description: Minneapolis : Lerner Publications, 2019. | Series: Sesame Street
    welcoming words | Includes bibliographical references.
Identifiers: LCCN 2018059331 (print) | LCCN 2019007809
    (ebook) | ISBN 9781541562523 (eb pdf) | ISBN 9781541555006 (lb : alk. paper) |
    ISBN 9781541574977 (pb : alk. paper)
Subjects:  LCSH: Spanish language—Conversation and phrase books—English—
    Juvenile literature.
Classification: LCC PC4121 (ebook) | LCC PC4121 .P74 2019 (print) |
    DDC 468.2/421—dc23
LC record available at https://lccn.loc.gov/2018059331

Manufactured in the United States of America
2-48800-42702-11/13/2019